SCIENCE
AND
RELIGION

POINT/COUNTERPOINT SERIES

Series Editor
James P. Sterba, University of Notre Dame

SCIENCE
AND
RELIGION

Are They Compatible?

Daniel C. Dennett
Alvin Plantinga

POINT/COUNTERPOINT SERIES
JAMES P. STERBA, SERIES EDITOR

New York   Oxford
OXFORD UNIVERSITY PRESS
2011

Oxford University Press, Inc., publishes works that further Oxford University's
objective of excellence in research, scholarship, and education.

Oxford   New York
Auckland   Cape Town   Dar es Salaam   Hong Kong   Karachi
Kuala Lumpur   Madrid   Melbourne   Mexico City   Nairobi
New Delhi   Shanghai   Taipei   Toronto

With offices in
Argentina   Austria   Brazil   Chile   Czech Republic   France   Greece
Guatemala   Hungary   Italy   Japan   Poland   Portugal   Singapore
South Korea   Switzerland   Thailand   Turkey   Ukraine   Vietnam

Copyright © 2011 by Oxford University Press, Inc.

Published by Oxford University Press, Inc.
198 Madison Avenue, New York, New York 10016
http://www.oup.com

Library of Congress Cataloging-in-Publication Data

Dennett, Daniel Clement.
   Science and religion : are they compatible? / Daniel C. Dennett,
Alvin Plantinga.
      p. cm.— (Point/counterpoint series)
   Includes bibliographical references and index.
   ISBN 978-0-19-973842-7
1. Religion and science.   I. Plantinga, Alvin.   II. Title.
   BL240.3.D46 2011
   201'.65—dc22   2010024690

9 8 7 6 5

Printed in the United States of America
on acid-free paper

CONTENTS

FOREWORD

It was the last time slot of the American Philosophical Association Central Division Meeting in Chicago for 2009. Sessions at that time slot for obvious reasons are usually not well attended, but this debate between Alvin Plantinga and Daniel Dennett was going to be different. As I approached the room assigned for the debate, I was redirected to a much larger room. Although I was still about ten minutes early, when I got to the new room all the seats had already been taken. I could have stood in the back or joined those who were beginning to fill the center aisle. Instead, I decided to walk to the very front of the room and found an empty spot just to the side of the speakers next to the wall. I couldn't have been closer.

Soon nearly all the floor space was occupied. The session was as well attended as a Presidential Address, and the room was abuzz with excitement, very different from a typical philosophy session. You could tell that people in attendance were expecting this to be a memorable event. And it was.

Plantinga began by narrowing the debate topic from "Are science and religion compatible?" to "Are contemporary evolutionary theory and the God of traditional Christian belief compatible?" He argued that not only is contemporary evolutionary theory compatible with the Christian God, but that it would be incredible to believe that "the wonders of the living world" resulted from an *unguided* evolution. In short, belief in evolutionary theory required belief in God.

Somewhat surprisingly, Dennett, at least initially, agreed with Plantinga that contemporary evolutionary theory and theistic belief were compatible. What Dennett strongly rejected, however, was the idea that unguided evolution was incredible or that belief in evolutionary theory required belief in God.

At various points in the debate, Superman, under different guises, the biochemist Michael Behe, and hand calculators, from simple to complex, were all used by Plantinga and Dennett to support their respective sides of the argument. When the debate concluded, no one really wanted it to be over.

So what we have done in this book is allow the debate to go on. First, we have reproduced the debate as it originally took place. Then, we have added a response of Dennett to Plantinga, another of Plantinga to Dennett, and a final response of Dennett to Plantinga. Hopefully, in this expanded version of the debate, one or the other of these distinguished philosophers will have succeeded in winning you over to his side of the argument.

James P. Sterba
Series Editor

ACKNOWLEDGMENTS

The authors of this book, along with Oxford University Press, would like to thank the following professors who provided useful feedback on this project: Robert M. Geraci at Manhattan College, Matt Lawrence at Long Beach City College, Michael L. Peterson at Asbury College, Gary Rosenkrantz at University of North Carolina at Greensboro, and several anonymous reviewers.

SCIENCE
AND
RELIGION

I

SCIENCE AND RELIGION

Where the Conflict Really Lies

Alvin Plantinga

Our question: Are science and religion compatible? A useful project would be to try to make the question more precise: What is religion? What is science? What is incompatibility, and what varieties does it come in (explicit contradiction, implicit contradiction, contradiction in the presence of plausible assumptions, improbability of their conjunction)? Some claim that theism is itself inconsistent, in which case, naturally enough, it will be incompatible with science (and everything else). Others retort that the same goes for science: Current general relativity is incompatible with current quantum theory, so that current science itself is inconsistent, in which case it is incompatible with religion (and everything else). These are good topics, but they'll have to wait for another occasion; here I'll assume that we have at least a rough grasp of the question. I won't be talking about religion generally, but about specifically theistic religion, in particular Christian belief; and when I speak of Christian belief, I'm thinking of C. S. Lewis's "mere Christianity," something like the intersection of the great Christian creeds. Although what I say is explicitly concerned with Christian belief, it will also be relevant to many versions of Judaism and Islam.

Why think there is conflict here? Many suggestions have been offered. Theistic religion endorses special divine action in the world—miracles, for example—but such action would contravene the laws promulgated by science. There is such a thing as the scientific worldview, and it is incompatible with theistic religion. Christian belief implies that human beings have been created in God's image, but contemporary evolutionary theory, properly understood, implies that neither God nor anyone else has designed, planned, or intended that human beings come to be. Evolutionary psychology is full of theories incompatible with theistic understandings of human beings. Some scientific historical Biblical scholarship argues that historical claims of Christianity, for example, that Jesus rose from the dead, are false or anyway groundless. These are all of great interest, but I'll limit myself, in this talk, to a cluster of issues having to do with evolution. I'll argue that (1) contemporary evolutionary theory is not incompatible with theistic belief; (2) the main anti-theistic arguments involving evolution together with other premises also fail; (3) even if current science, evolutionary or otherwise, were incompatible with theistic belief, it wouldn't follow that theistic belief is irrational or unwarranted or in any other kind of trouble; and finally, (4) naturalism, the thought that there is no such thing as the God of theistic religion or anything like him, is an essential element in the naturalistic worldview, which is a sort of quasi-religion in the sense that it plays some of the most important roles of religion; the naturalistic worldview is in fact incompatible with evolution. Hence there is a science-religion (or science–quasi-religion) conflict, all right, but it is a conflict between naturalism and science, not theistic religion and science.

I. Contemporary Evolutionary Theory Is Compatible with Theistic Belief

The term *evolution* covers a variety of theses: (1) the ancient earth thesis; (2) the thesis of descent with modification, that is, the thought that the enormous diversity of the contemporary living world has come about by way of offspring differing, ordinarily in small and subtle ways, from their parents; and (3) the common ancestry thesis: the claim that, as Gould put it, there is a "tree of evolutionary descent linking all organisms by ties of genealogy."[1] I'll use the term *evolution* to refer to the conjunction of these three. There is also (4) the claim that the principle mechanism driving this process of descent with modification is natural selection winnowing random genetic mutation. Since a similar proposal was characteristic of Darwin ("Natural selection has been the main but not exclusive means of modification"), call this thesis Darwinism. It's clear, I think, that there is no conflict between theistic religion and the ancient earth thesis, or the descent with modification thesis, or the common ancestry thesis. According to theistic belief, God has created the living world; but of course he could have done so in many different ways, and in particular in ways compatible with those theses. What about the fourth thesis, Darwinism? Is *it* incompatible with theistic religion?

Many apparently think so: Among them are Richard Dawkins, Daniel Dennett, George Gaylord Simpson, and many others, and far to the other side, Philip Johnson. But are they right? Where, exactly, would the incompatibility arise? A suggested source of conflict has to do with the Christian doctrine of creation, in particular the claim that God has created human beings *in his image.* This requires that God *intended* to create creatures of a certain kind and *planned that there be* creatures of that kind—rational creatures with a moral sense and the capacity to know and love him—and then acted in such a way as to accomplish this intention. This claim is clearly consistent with evolution, as conservative Christian theologians have pointed out as far back as 1871.[2] But is it also consistent with Darwinism? It looks as if it is. God could have caused the right mutations to arise at the right time, he could have preserved populations from perils of various sorts, and so on; in this way, by orchestrating the course of evolution, he could have ensured that there come to be creatures of the kind he intends.

What is *not* consistent with Christian belief, however, is the claim that evolution and Darwinism are *unguided*— where I'll take that to include *being unplanned and unintended.* What is not consistent with Christian belief is the claim that no personal agent, not even God, has guided, planned, intended, directed, orchestrated, or shaped this whole process. Yet precisely this claim is made by a large number of contemporary scientists and philosophers who write on this topic. There is a veritable choir of extremely distinguished experts insisting that this process is unguided, and indeed insisting that it is a part of contemporary evolutionary theory to assert that it is unguided, so that evolutionary theory as such is incompatible with Christian belief. According to George Gaylord Simpson, for example, "Man [and no doubt woman as well] is the result of a purposeless and natural process that did not have him in mind."[3] In this connection the late Stephen J. Gould and others have emphasized what they take to be the chancy, contingent, and undirected character of evolution; if the evolutionary tape were to be rewound and then let go forward again, the chances are we'd get creatures of very different sorts from the ones actually present on earth. The chances are we'd get nothing much like *Homo sapiens.* But Gould's suggestion *presupposes* that God has not guided and orchestrated the course of evolution, and hence can't be appealed to as a reason for supposing that he has not done so. Given the biological evidence and the proposition that God has indeed created human beings in his image, Gould's suggestion is wholly implausible; for if the tape were rewound and let go forward again, no doubt God would still have intended that there be creatures created in his image, and would still have seen to it that there be such creatures.

What about the fact that the relevant genetic mutations are said to be *random?* You might wonder whether genetic mutations could be both random and intended and caused by God: If these mutations are random, aren't they just a matter of chance, blind chance? But it is no part of current evolutionary theory to say that these mutations are random in a sense implying that they are uncaused (they are said to be caused by cosmic rays, for example); still less that they occur just by chance. According to Ernst Mayr, the dean of post–World War II biology, "When it is said that mutation or variation is random, the statement simply means that there is no correlation between the production of new genotypes and the adaptational needs of an organism in the given environment."[4] Elliott Sober puts the point a bit more carefully: "There is no *physical mechanism* (either inside organisms or outside of them) that detects which mutations would be beneficial and causes those mutations to occur."[5] The point is that a mutation accruing to an organism is random just if neither the organism nor its environment contains a mechanism or process or organ that causes adaptive mutations to occur. But clearly a mutation could be both random in that sense and also intended and indeed caused by God.

Hence the randomness involved in Darwinism does not imply that the process is not divinely guided. The fact, if it is a fact, that human beings have come to be by way of natural selection operating on random genetic mutation is not at all incompatible with their having been designed by God and created in his image. Therefore Darwinism is perfectly compatible with God's guiding, orchestrating, and overseeing the whole process. Indeed, it is perfectly compatible with that idea that God *causes* the random genetic mutations that are winnowed by natural selection. Those who claim that evolution shows that humankind and other living things have not been designed apparently confuse a naturalistic gloss on the scientific theory with the theory itself. The claim that evolution demonstrates that human beings and other living creatures have not, contrary to appearances, been designed, is not part of or a consequence of the scientific theory as such, but a metaphysical or theological add-on.[6] Naturalism implies, of course, that we human beings have not been designed and created in God's image (because it implies that there is no God); but evolutionary science by itself does not carry this implication. Naturalism and evolutionary theory *together* imply the denial of divine design, but evolutionary theory *by itself* doesn't have that implication. It is only evolutionary science *combined with naturalism* that implies this denial. Since naturalism all by itself has this implication, it is no surprise that when you conjoin it with science or, as far as that goes, anything else—the complete works of William McGonagall or the *Farmer's Almanac,* or the Apostle's Creed—the conjunction will also have this implication.

II. Broader Anti-theistic Arguments from Evolution

Darwinism as such doesn't include or imply the proposition that the process is unguided; what about broader anti-theistic arguments involving evolution? I'm aware of three sorts of arguments proposed here. First, there is the claim that evolution undercuts the argument from design, thus reducing the rational support, if any, enjoyed by theism. Second, there is the suggestion that the process of evolution, so wasteful and productive of suffering, is not the sort of process God would use or permit. And third, there is the thought that unguided evolution, as a hypothesis, is superior to the hypothesis that the process of evolution has been guided or orchestrated by mind, divine or otherwise, because it is simpler and more Ockhamistic. None of these objections, I believe, is promising. While I can't deal properly with any or all of them in the time allotted to me, I'll briefly outline a response to each.

Start with the claim that evolution undercuts the argument from design, thus making it less reasonable to accept theistic belief. According to John Dupré, "Darwinism undermines the only remotely plausible reason for believing in the existence of God"—that is, the argument from design.[7]

Now it's reasonable to think that evolution makes it somewhat easier to be rational or sensible in accepting atheism; prior to 1859 there simply weren't decent answers to the question, "If this abundant variety of life wasn't created by God, how did it get here?" But making it easier to be a rational atheist doesn't as such make it harder to be a rational theist, and doesn't as such create a religion–science conflict. And how much support does the argument from design actually offer theistic belief? Perhaps it supports belief in the existence of a very powerful, very knowledgeable being or group of beings, but that's a long way from theism.

In any event, however, current molecular biology may offer the materials for a different sort of argument from design, as explained in the much maligned Michael Behe's recent book, *The Edge of Evolution*.[8] His argument is one of the few serious and quantitative arguments in this area. We have the living cell, both prokaryotic and eukaryotic, with its stupifying complexity and its multitude of elaborately complex protein machines.[9] Behe argues that unguided natural selection is probably incapable of producing these protein machines. His argument is quantitative and empirical rather than a priori; its centerpiece is the saga of the malaria parasite, *Plasmodium falciperum,* and its long trench warfare with the human genome. I don't have the space here to outline his argument; but to me as a layman, the argument seems reasonably powerful, though far from conclusive. If Behe is right, or anywhere near right, the probability of the existence of the cell as we find it is much greater on theism than on naturalism. And if this is so, the argument from design is reinstated at a deeper level. What current biological science takes away with one hand, it restores with the other.

But the real point lies in a different direction. Belief in God is seldom accepted on the basis of the teleological argument, or indeed any argument or propositional evidence at all. Both untutored observation and current research in the scientific study of religion suggest that a tendency to believe in God or something like God, apart from any propositional evidence, is part of our native cognitive endowment. Furthermore, if theistic belief is true, it probably doesn't require propositional evidence for its *rational* acceptance. As I argue in *Warranted Christian Belief,* if theistic belief is true, then very likely it has both rationality and warrant in the *basic* way, that is, not on the basis of propositional evidence. If theistic belief is true, then very likely there is a cognitive structure something like John Calvin's *sensus divinitatis,* an original source of warranted theistic belief. In this way belief in God, like belief in other minds, has its own source of rationality and warrant, and doesn't depend on argument from other sources for those estimable qualities. The demise of the teleological argument, if indeed evolution has compromised it, is little more of a threat to rational belief in God than the demise of the argument from analogy for other minds is to rational belief in other minds.

Second, there is the suggestion, made by Gould and others, that the waste and suffering involved in evolution is evidence against theism. Philip Kitcher puts it like this: "When we envisage a human analogue presiding over a miniaturized version of the arrangement—it's hard to equip the face with a kindly expression." He goes on to suggest that "had a benevolent creator proposed to use evolution under natural selection as a means for attaining his purposes, we could have given him some useful advice."[10] I don't know how such advice would be received, but of course we don't require evolutionary theory or current science to tell us that the animal world is full of predation, death, pain, and suffering. Alfred Tennyson noted that "nature is red in tooth and claw"[11] well before 1859, and no doubt some suspected this even earlier. Still, current science gives us reason to believe that suffering and death have afflicted the human and animal world for a much longer time than was ordinarily thought before the nineteenth century. It has therefore given us information about the extent and duration of animal suffering, including human suffering.

The first thing to see is that this is a special case of the so-called problem of evil, a problem alleged to afflict theistic belief. Sin and suffering do indeed constitute a problem or perplexity for theism, although it may be hard to specify precisely what this problem is. Most atheist thinkers have given up the idea that the existence of sin and suffering is logically incompatible with theistic belief; some kind of inductive or probabilistic anti-theistic argument is presumably what's at issue. It has proven surprisingly difficult, however, to give a plausible statement of a probabilistic argument from evil,[12] and as these arguments become more complex, they also become less convincing. Surely, however, sin and suffering and evil present *some* kind of problem or at least perplexity for theists; the existence of so much suffering and hurt in God's world certainly seems to call out for an explanation of some sort. And what current biological science adds to the problem is that predation, suffering, and death have been going on for a very long time. But does this put any additional pressure on the various theistic or Christian responses to suffering and evil?

My own favorite response is the "O Felix Culpa" response, according to which all of the really good possible worlds involve divine incarnation and atonement, or at any rate atonement.[13] But then all the best possible worlds also involve a great deal of sin and as a consequence a great deal of suffering. Some of this suffering is on the part of nonhuman creatures. Christians think of suffering, both human and nonhuman, as due in one way or another to sin, although not necessarily to human sin; there are also Satan and his minions, who may, as C. S. Lewis suggests, be involved in one way or another in the evolution of the nonhuman living world. But learning that sin and suffering have been going on for much longer than we originally thought shouldn't raise an additional difficulty for the "O Felix Culpa" response. Suppose we learn that our world, with all its problems, heartaches, and cruelty, will endure for millions of years before the advent of the New Heaven and the New Earth; that wouldn't have much bearing, so one thinks, on the viability or satisfactoriness of this response to evil. (The New Heaven and the New Earth, after all, will exist for a vastly longer period than our current sad and troubled old world.) But the same goes, I should think, for our learning that our world, with all the ills it is heir to, has gone on for much longer than originally thought. Current science shows that suffering, both human and animal, has gone on much longer than previously thought; but it doesn't thereby diminish the value of Christian responses to the problem of evil and in this way doesn't exacerbate that problem much, if at all.

Finally, there is the claim, perhaps made more often in the oral tradition than in print, that the hypothesis of unguided evolution is simpler, more in accord with Ockhamistic injunctions, than the hypothesis that God or other intelligent beings have shaped and guided the course of terrestrial evolution. Here two points are relevant. First, even if unguided evolution is more Ockhamistic than guided evolution, it isn't at all clear that the former is all-things-considered superior, as a hypothesis, to the latter. It involves fewer kinds of beings, yes, but that isn't the only relevant consideration. Another is their respective likelihoods, the probabilities of the living world (more exactly, its variety) coming to be by way of these two hypotheses. Let D be the proposition that the variety of the living world has come to be by Darwinian processes, E the relevant biological evidence, G the proposition that evolution is guided, and U the proposition that it is unguided. Then our question is which is greater: $P(D/E\&G)$ or $P(D/E\&U)$?[14] It is, of course, overwhelmingly difficult to make anything like reasonably precise judgments here, but perhaps we can make sensible comparative judgments. Consider first $P(D/E\&G)$. Clearly God could have created living things by way of natural selection, causing the right mutations to arise at the right time, preserving the relevant populations from disaster, and the like; he could also have allowed other intelligent creatures to be involved in the whole process. Again, it is overwhelmingly difficult to estimate the probability that this is the way in which it has in fact happened; but $P(D/E\&G)$ is perhaps not terribly low.

What about $P(D/E\&U)$? Going all the way back to St. George Mivart, critics have expressed serious doubts as to whether the eye, for example, could have come to be by way of unguided natural selection operating on random genetic mutation—could have, that is, apart from absolutely stunning improbability. The eye, the mammalian brain, and other organs remain difficult problems for unguided evolution. But the really hard problem here for unguided Darwinists isn't the development of macroscopic organs such as eyes and hearts. The hard problem is rather at the microscopic (molecular) level: the stupefying complexity[15] of the living cell, both prokaryotic and eukaryotic. It's only in the last half-century or so that this enormous complexity has come into view; the eminent scientist Ernst Haeckel summed up nineteenth-century opinion when he declared the cell "a simple little lump of albuminous combination of carbon."[16]

Of course it is widely assumed that in fact the cell *must* have come to be in that fashion; but there is little by way of serious argument for the conclusion that its thus coming to be is less than prohibitively improbable. On the other hand, as I said above, Michael Behe has proposed a serious and quantitative argument for the opposite conclusion.[17] Given the stunning complexity of the living cell with its enormous complication, together with what we know about mutation rates, the age of the earth, population sizes, and the like, it seems reasonable to estimate that P(D/E&U) is exceedingly low, orders of magnitude lower than P(D/E&G). If this is right, then even if we think U, as an explanation, is Ockhamistically superior to G, it is inferior to G in that the relevant likelihood is lower.

But again, the real point lies in a different direction. The theistic noetic structure already, of course, includes the existence of God. Relative to that noetic structure, therefore, there is no additional Ockhamistic cost in the hypothesis of guided evolution. As an analogy, suppose we land a spaceship on a planet we know is inhabited by intelligent creatures. We find something that looks exactly like a stone arrowhead, complete with grooves and indentations apparently made in the process of shaping and sharpening it. Two possibilities suggest themselves: one, that it acquired these characteristics by way of erosion, let's say, and the other, that it was intentionally designed and fashioned by the inhabitants. Someone with a couple of courses in philosophy might suggest that the former hypothesis is to be preferred because it posits fewer entities than the latter. He'd be wrong, of course; since we already know that the planet contains intelligent creatures, there is no Ockhamistic cost involved in thinking those structures designed. The same would go for evolution; theists already accept divine design, and do not incur additional Ockhamistic cost by way of thinking of evolution as guided.

This objection to guided evolution would have more by way of teeth if we, theist and atheist alike, were starting from an agnostic position, and then the theist proposed to postulate the existence of a divine designer to explain the course of evolution. That would be substantially like offering a theistic argument; and then the availability of a nontheistic alternative hypothesis, provided the relevant likelihood wasn't too overwhelmingly small, would undercut the argument. But of course in this context the theist isn't presenting a theistic argument. She already accepts divine design; hence the fact that guided evolution involves more entities than unguided evolution is no reason in favor of the latter. Since that is so, there is no conflict here between theistic religion and evolutionary science.

I've argued that the contemporary scientific theory of evolution (taken as including Darwinism) does not entail the claim that natural selection is unguided. But suppose

I'm mistaken, or suppose instead that current evolutionary theory itself evolves in such a way that this claim becomes part of it. This could certainly happen. We can easily imagine the authorities and the textbooks stating the theory in such a way as to explicitly include the claim that natural selection is unguided by any personal agent; after all, many, probably most biologists believe that it *is* unguided. Would that show that there is scientific evidence against theism? Hardly. We could imagine physics evolving in the same direction: all the physics textbooks unite in endorsing general relativity, adding that the behavior of large-scale physical systems is never guided by any personal agents. In neither case, obviously, would it follow that there is scientific evidence against theism. Annexing a proposition *p* to one for which there is evidence doesn't automatically confer evidence on *p*. I learn that Feike is a Frisian lifeguard; that increases the probability that he can swim, and also the probability of the proposition *Feike can swim and the next toss of this coin will land heads;* it does not increase the probability that *the next toss of this coin will land heads.*

And even if, contrary to fact, there were scientific evidence for unguided evolution and hence for atheism, that would by no means settle the issue. Suppose there is scientific evidence against theism: it doesn't follow that theism is false, or that theists have a defeater for their beliefs, or that theistic belief is irrational, or in some other way problematic. Perhaps there is also evidence, scientific or otherwise, *for* theism. But second, and more important, as I mentioned, if theism is true, it is likely that it has its own intrinsic and basic source of warrant—something like the *sensus divinitatis* proposed by John Calvin, or the natural but confused knowledge of God proposed by Thomas Aquinas.[18] If so, the warrant for theistic belief doesn't depend on the state of current science. Indeed, what Christians and other theists should think of current science can quite properly depend, in part, on theology. For example, science has not spoken with a single voice about the question of whether the universe has a beginning: First the idea was that it did, but then the steady state theory triumphed, but then Big Bang cosmology achieved ascendancy, but now there are straws in the wind suggesting a reversion to the thought that the universe is without a beginning. The sensible Christian believer is not obliged to trim her sails to the current scientific breeze on this topic, revising her belief on the topic every time science changes its mind; if the most satisfactory Christian (or theistic) theology endorses the idea that the universe did indeed have a beginning (isn't eternal), the believer has a perfect right to accept that thought. If so, then even if there were scientific evidence against theism, and no propositional evidence, scientific or otherwise, in favor of it, it might still be both rational and warranted.

III. Naturalism vs. Evolution

Naturalism comes in more than one variety. Here, as I said, I take it to be the view that there is no such person as the God of theistic religion nor anything like God. So taken, naturalism is not a religion. Nevertheless it is a crucial part of the naturalistic worldview, which in turn plays at least one of the most important roles of a religion. This worldview functions as a sort of myth, in a technical sense of that term: It offers a way of interpreting ourselves to ourselves, a way of understanding our origin and significance at the deep level of religion. It tells us where we come from, what our prospects are, what our place in the universe is, whether there is life after death, and the like. We could therefore say that it is a "quasi-religion." What I propose to argue next is that naturalism and current science are incompatible, so that there is a religion (or quasi-religion) conflict, sure enough, but it is between science and naturalism, not science and theistic religion. What I'll argue is that naturalism is incompatible with evolution, in the sense that one can't rationally accept them both. Since I've given this argument elsewhere, here I can be brief.

First, note that naturalists are all or nearly all materialists about human persons; a human person is a material object through and through, with no immaterial self or soul or subject. For present purposes, therefore, I'll assimilate materialism to naturalism. The central premises of the argument are as follows. Where N is naturalism, E is current evolutionary theory and R is the proposition that our cognitive faculties are reliable,

1. $P(R/N\&E)$ is low.[19]
2. One who accepts N&E and also sees that 1 is true has a defeater for R.
3. This defeater can't be defeated.
4. One who has a defeater for R has a defeater for any belief she takes to be produced by her cognitive faculties, including N&E.

Therefore

5. N&E is self-defeating and can't rationally be accepted.

These premises need defense, perhaps the first one in particular. So suppose there are beliefs; this isn't essential to the argument for premise 1, but it will facilitate brief statement of it. From the point of view of materialism, a belief will presumably be an event or structure in the nervous system, perhaps in the brain. It will be a structure involving many neurons connected in various ways. This structure will respond to input from other such structures, from sense organs, and the like; it may also send signals along effector nerves to muscles and glands, thereby causing behavior. Such a structure will have at least two kinds of properties: On the one hand, it will have neurophysiological properties (NP properties) specifying, for example, the number of neurons involved in the structure, the rate of fire in various parts of it, the change in rate of fire in one part in response to change of rate of fire in another, the way in which it is connected with other structures and with muscles, and so on. But if it is a *belief,* it will also have a property of a quite different sort, a mental property: It will have a content; it will be the belief that *p,* for some proposition *p.*

NP properties are physical properties; *having such and such a content* is a mental property. There are three ways in which, given materialism, mental and physical properties can be related. First, nonreductive materialism: While mental properties can't be reduced to physical properties, they *supervene* on them. (Take supervenience as follows: Properties of sort *A* supervene on properties of sort *B* just if necessarily, if entities *x* and *y* differ with respect to their A properties, then they differ with respect to their B properties.) The necessity involved can be either broadly logical (metaphysical) necessity, or nomological necessity, giving us two varieties of supervenience, logical and nomological, and hence two possibilities as to the relation of mental properties to physical properties. The third possibility for that relation is reductive materialism: Every mental property is identical with some physical property.

To avoid interspecific chauvinism, suppose we think not about ourselves, but about a population of creatures, perhaps in one of those other cosmoi proposed by inflationary scenarios, who resemble us in holding beliefs, changing beliefs, making inferences, and so on. Suppose also that naturalism holds for these creatures, and that they have come to be by the processes specified in contemporary evolutionary theory. Now ask about P(R/N&E) specified, not to us, but to them; and consider that probability with respect to each of the preceding three suggestions about the relation of mental and physical properties. Consider first logical nonreductive materialism (LNM): Mental properties are distinct from physical properties, but supervene upon them, where the necessity involved is broadly logical. What is P(R/N&E&LNM)? These creatures have evolved; we may therefore assume that their behavior is adaptive, in their circumstances, and that, accordingly, the neurophysiology producing that behavior is also adaptive. But natural selection doesn't give a fig for true belief just as such. It rewards adaptive behavior and punishes maladaptive behavior, but it doesn't care about truth of belief; as Patricia Churchland says, "Truth, whatever that is, definitely takes the hindmost."[20] So choose any particular belief B held by one of those creatures. We may assume that B is adaptive in that its NP properties are adaptive; but of course nothing follows about the truth or falsehood of the content that supervenes on those properties. If the supervening content is true, excellent; but if it is false, that's just as good. Its falsehood in no way interferes with the adaptivity of the NP properties. We should assume, therefore, that the probability of that belief's being true, given N&E and nonreductive logical supervenience, is about .5. But then the probability of their faculties being reliable will be low. If you have 100 independent beliefs and the probability of each is .5, the probability that three-fourths of them are true, which is a modest requirement for reliability, will be less than one out of a million.

P(R/N&E&LNM), therefore, is low.

But of course the very same thing will hold, for the same reasons, for P(R/N&E&NNM), where NNM is the version of non-reductive materialism where mental properties supervene upon physical properties with nomological necessity. That leaves reductive materialism (RM). What is P(R/N&E&RM)? Here the property of having such and such a content is identical with some physical, presumably neurological property. Again, consider any particular belief *B* held by one of those creatures. We may suppose that having *B* is adaptive, and adaptive by virtue of its content as well as its other physical properties. But once again, it doesn't matter whether the content associated with *B* is true or false. We may assume that the physical property identical with the property of having *B's* content is adaptive; the content associated with *B* is of course either true or false; if it happens to be false, this in no way compromises the adaptivity of *B*. Once more, then, we must suppose that the probability of that belief's being true is about .5; but then it will be unlikely that the cognitive faculties of these creatures are reliable.

It follows, therefore, that P(R/N&E) with respect to these hypothetical creatures is low. But then of course the same goes for us; P(R/N&E) is low for us as well. The next step is to note that anyone who sees that P(R/N&E) is low, and also accepts N&E, has a defeater for R in her own case, a reason for rejecting R, for giving it up, for no longer believing it. This defeater cannot itself be defeated; that is because a defeater for this defeater would have to take the form of an argument. But of course one who accepts N&E will also have a defeater for the premises of this argument, as well as the proposition that if the premises are true, so is the conclusion. Another way to put it: Any argument for R will be epistemically circular, in that reliance on the argument presupposes that the conclusion of the argument is true.

But anyone who has a defeater for R has a defeater for any belief she takes to be produced by her cognitive faculties—including, of course, N&E itself. Hence one who accepts N&E (and sees the truth of the first premise) has a defeater for N&E; N&E, therefore, is self-defeating and cannot rationally be accepted. If so, however, there is a conflict between naturalism and evolution; their conjunction cannot rationally be accepted. Evolution, however, is one of the pillars of contemporary science. Hence there is a science–religion or perhaps science–quasi-religion conflict in the neighborhood of evolution, all right, but not between evolution and theistic religion. The real conflict is between evolution, that pillar of contemporary science, and *naturalism*.[21]

NOTES

1. Stephen Jay Gould, *Hen's Teeth and Horse's Toes* (New York: W.W. Norton, 1983), 236.
2. Thus Charles Hodge, the distinguished Princeton theologian, speaking of the design of plants and animals, "If God made them, it makes no difference how He made them, as far as the question of design is concerned, whether at once or by a process of evolution." Charles Hodge, *What Is Darwinism?* (New York: Charles Scribner, 1871), 44.

3. George Gaylord Simpson, *The Meaning of Evolution* (New Haven, CT: Yale University Press, rev. ed., 1967), 344–45.

4. Ernest Mayr, *Toward a New Philosophy of Biology: Observations of an Evolutionist* (Cambridge, MA: Harvard University Press, 1988), 99.

5. Elliott Sober, "Evolution Without Metaphysics?"

6. I don't mean to suggest that no scientific theory can contain metaphysical elements. The suggestion is only that this particular claim is clearly metaphysical, and also clearly an add-on: It isn't part of evolutionary theory as currently stated and understood.

7. John Dupré, *Darwin's Legacy: What Evolution Means Today* (Oxford, UK: Oxford University Press, 2003), 56.

8. Michael Behe, *The Edge of Evolution: The Search for the Limits of Darwinism* (New York: Free Press, 2007).

9. See Bruce Alberts, "The Cell as a Collection of Protein Machines: Preparing the Next Generation of Molecular Biologists," *Cell*, 92: 291–94.

10. Philip Kitcher, "The Conflict Between Science and Religion," in *The Blackwell Guide to the Philosophy of Religion*, ed. William E. Mann (Oxford, UK: Blackwell, 2005), 268.

11. Alfred Tennyson "In Memoriam A. H. H.," *Alfred Lord Tennyson: Selected Poems*, canto 56, 135.

12. See, for example, William Rowe, "The Evidential Argument from Evil: A Second Look," in *The Evidential Argument from Evil*, ed. Daniel Howard-Snyder (Bloomington: Indiana University Press, 1996), and Michael Tooley's statement of the argument in Alvin Plantinga and Michael Tooley, *Knowledge of God* (Malden, MA: Blackwell, 2008), 98ff.

13. See Alvin Plantinga, "Superlapsarianism, or 'O Felix Culpa,'" in *Christian Faith and the Problem of Evil*, ed. Peter van Inwagen (Grand Rapids, MI: Eerdmans, 1994).

14. "P(D/E&G)" and "P(D/E&U)" are to be read as "the probability of D, given E and G" and "the probability of D, given E and U."

15. Thus, according to Bruce Alberts, President of the National Academy of Sciences, "Nearly every process in a cell is carried out by assemblies of 10 or more protein molecules.... Indeed, the entire cell can be viewed as a factory that contains an elaborate network of interacting assembly lines, each of which is composed of a set of large protein machines." Alberts, "The Cell as a Collection of Protein Machines: Preparing the Next Generation of Molecular Biologists," 291.

16. Ernst Haeckel, in John Farley, *The Spontaneous Generation Controversy from Descartes to Oparin*, 2nd ed. (Baltimore, MD: The Johns Hopkins Univ. Press, 1977), 73.

17. Behe, *The Edge of Evolution*.

18. See Alvin Plantinga, *Warranted Christian Belief* (New York: Oxford University Press, 2000), part III, especially ch. 8 and 9.

19. "P(R/N&E)" is to be read as "the probability of R, given N and E."

20. Patricia Churchland, *Journal of Philosophy* (LXXXIV, Oct. 1987), 548.

21. Thanks to Nathan Ballantyne, Mike Bergmann, Brian Boeninger, Tom Crisp, Eric Hagedorn, Matthew Lee, Trenton Merricks, Anne Peterson, Josh Rasmussen, Luke Van Horn, Rene van Woudenberg, and especially Michael Rea.

2

TRUTHS THAT MISS THEIR MARK

Naturalism Unscathed

Daniel C. Dennett

I am going to show that three of Professor Plantinga's central claims are right, but only in senses that fail to support his larger project.

I. "Contemporary evolutionary theory is compatible with theistic belief."

II. "[I]t is no part of current evolutionary theory to say that...mutations are random in a sense implying...that they occur just by chance."

26   Science and Religion: Are They Compatible?

III. "Naturalism and evolutionary theory *together* imply the denial of divine design, but evolutionary biology *by itself* doesn't have that implication."

I. "Contemporary evolutionary theory is compatible with theistic belief."

Plantinga is right about this, given the way he defines his terms, and lurking within his claim is an important point I have often stressed myself, since I first expressed it in 1990.

> In our world today, there are organisms we know to be the result of foresighted, goal-seeking redesign efforts, but that knowledge depends on our direct knowledge of recent historical events (we've actually watched the breeders at work), but these special events might not cast any fossily shadows into the future. To take a simpler variation on our thought experiment, suppose we were to send Martian biologists a laying hen, a Pekingese dog, a barn swallow, and a cheetah and ask them to determine which designs bore the mark of intervention by artificial selectors. What could they rely on? How would they argue? They might note that the hen did not care "properly" for her eggs; some varieties of hen have had their instinct for broodiness bred right out of them, and would soon become extinct were it not for the environment of artificial incubators human beings have provided for them. They might note that the Pekingese was pathetically ill suited for fending for itself in any demanding environment. The barn swallow's fondness for carpentered nest sites might fool them into the view that it was some sort of pet, and whatever features of the cheetah convinced them that it was a creature of the wild might also be found in greyhounds, and have been patiently encouraged by breeders. Artificial environments are themselves a part of nature, after all.
>
> Prehistoric fiddling by intergalactic visitors with the DNA of earthly species cannot be ruled out, except on

grounds that it is an entirely gratuitous fantasy. Nothing we have found (so far) on earth so much as hints that such a hypothesis is worth further exploration. (And note—I hasten to add, lest creationists take heart—that even if we were to discover and translate such a "trademark message" in our spare DNA, this would do nothing to rescind the claim of the theory of natural selection to explain all design in nature without invocation of a foresighted Designer-Creator outside the system. If the theory of evolution by natural selection can account for the existence of the people at NovaGene who dreamt up DNA branding, it can also account for the existence of any predecessors who may have left their signatures around for us to discover.) The power of the theory of natural selection is not the power to prove exactly how (pre-)history was, but only the power to prove how it could have been, given what we know about how things are.[1]

So I agree that contemporary evolutionary theory can't *demonstrate* the absence of intelligent design, and any biologist who insists that we can is overstating the case. But Plantinga must deal with the implications of one sentence in the passage above: "Prehistoric fiddling by intergalactic visitors with the DNA of earthly species cannot be ruled out, except on grounds that *it is an entirely gratuitous fantasy*" (emphasis added). Now we might draw the debate to a close right here. I could happily concede that anybody who wishes to entertain the fantasy that intelligent designers from another galaxy (or another dimension) fiddled with our evolutionary prehistory, or salted Earth with life forms, or even arranged for the constants of physics to take on their particular "local" values will find their fantasy consistent with contemporary evolutionary biology. There is not a shred of evidence for any such fantasy, but it's a free country, and it might be harmless enough to keep such fairy tales alive, but in general, I think, it is wise of us not to respect such frivolities, since they can, in fact, do serious damage to the epistemological fabric of our society. For instance, they might mislead deluded people into basing policy on them, for instance, by offering public sacrifices to those imagined intelligent designers in hopes of enticing them to return and repair our damaged planet, or, to take two entirely real and utterly deplorable examples, they might mislead deluded people into dismissing environmental concerns since the End Times will soon be upon us in any case, or spawn hatred of a political candidate because he is deemed to be the Antichrist. (I call on all Christians to speak out publicly and explicitly to dismiss as pernicious nonsense such obscene creeds, which have an altogether worrying grip on the popular imagination of too many of our fellow citizens.)

Perhaps, you think, Plantinga's theistic creed is in better position than any science-fictional fantasy. Let us consider, for concreteness's sake, a candidate. Superman, son of Jor-el, also later known as Clark Kent, came from the planet Krypton about 530 million years ago and ignited the Cambrian explosion. Superman "could have caused the right mutations to arise at the right time, he could have preserved populations from perils of various sorts, and so on; in this way, by orchestrating the course of evolution, he could have ensured that there come to be creatures of the kind he intends" (Plantinga, p. 4).

Superman, according to my hypothesis, seeded a handy planet so that in the fullness of time he could have playthings, a sort of Super Ken and Barbie World. A rather adolescent project, perhaps, but nevertheless a motivated instance of intelligent design.

Now the burden of proof falls on Plantinga to show why his theist story deserves any more respect or credence than this one. I myself cannot see any rational grounds for preferring his theism over my Supermanism—which I don't espouse, but see as perfectly consistent with contemporary evolutionary theory. Moreover, I can describe experiments that *could* make my Superman hypothesis highly probable if they panned out.

Here's a crude example: We drill and dynamite a big crater in the Burgess Shale, and thereby expose, for the first time in over half a billion years, a set of golden plates, not the Angel Moroni's golden plates, but Jor-el's golden plates, which, unlike Moroni's, don't conveniently disappear, and are soon carefully studied by the National Academy of Sciences. The inscriptions on them prove to be instructions from Jor-el to his son, explaining how to ensure that the intended gene duplications occur to hasten the path to new body plans, the evolution of vision, and eventually of vertebrates.

Of course it is just as true that tomorrow the clouds could part, and a giant voice could boom out in all the languages of the world simultaneously, saying "I, Allah, of whom Muhammad is the prophet, have been intervening in evolution for billions of years on this little planet." I wonder if Plantinga would say, "You see? You see? I was right!"

II. Plantinga is right that "it is no part of current evolutionary theory to say that... mutations are random in a sense implying that they are uncaused (they are said to be caused by cosmic rays, for example); still less that they occur just by chance."

This is often misunderstood. As I pointed out in *Elbow Room*,[2] even so great an evolutionist as Nobel Laureate Jacques Monod could make the mistake of thinking that evolution could not occur in "Laplace's world, from which chance is excluded by definition."[3] Evolution can occur just fine in deterministic worlds, as thousands of deterministic computer models of evolution demonstrate on a daily basis (they are all deterministic, relying on pseudo-random number generators as their source of "random" mutation). Indeterminism is indeed a red herring, both for evolution and for free will, as I have argued for decades.

III. Plantinga's largest claim is that "Naturalism and evolutionary theory *together* imply the denial of divine design, but evolutionary biology *by itself* doesn't have that implication."

This is also true, but in its own special way, which I illustrate with a parallel story:

> Fred the nasty art critic has published a scathing review of an exhibit of Tom's art, and is found dead in his apartment the next day, his head bashed in by one of Tom's sculptures, which lies soaked in blood beside the corpse, with the published review draped over the body. Murder most foul, it appears, but at Tom's trial the defense is impressive: The sculpture in question had belonged to Fred for years, and can be seen perched precariously on the high shelf above his reading chair in a photograph taken a week earlier. Moreover, that morning shortly after 9, at which time Fred habitually read the morning paper, a moderate earthquake (see the evidence here on the seismograph) had shaken all the houses in the neighborhood. Many similar items were jiggled off shelves and tables in the neighborhood that day, and there was no evidence that Tom was anywhere nearby: no sign of breaking and entering, no fingerprints, no DNA, etc. In all likelihood, Fred's death was *by natural causes, not a murder, not a death with an intending and intelligent author.*

Tom's acquittal now seems assured, but the prosecutor isn't finished; he calls an expert witness, Professor Plantinga.

"Do you believe Tom murdered Fred?"

"Yes I do."

"But hasn't the defense shown that it was an accident, a death by natural causes, not a murder?"

"No, the defense has shown, I grant, that it *could* have been an accident, but not that it *was* an accident. There is no inconsistency between the case that the defense has made and the proposition, which I find entirely reasonable, that Tom was the deliberate author of Fred's death."

"Do you deny that there was an earthquake sufficient to topple the sculpture?"

"No, but Tom could have arranged for the earthquake to happen just so! Nothing we know in geology *by itself* rules out the possibility that people can cause earthquakes by wishing for them hard enough. Or, as I have said, 'Satan and his minions'...may be involved in one way or another."

"But..."

"I grant you that *naturalism* combined with what we know of geology has the implication that Fred's death was almost certainly not a murder, but naturalism has not been established or even defended in this court."

Of course not, because naturalism is *tacitly assumed* in all reputable courts of law, and throughout scientific investigation.

As Plantinga makes clear, naturalism is the creed he wants to discredit. This puts him in an awkward position. If he wants to champion the "much maligned" Michael Behe, he needs to make his peace with naturalism. Behe's so-called scientific work has been carefully judged by the scientific community and thoroughly rejected. The last thing Michael Behe needs is a defender who insists that naturalism is not to be assumed for the sake of argument. Without naturalism Behe is just another theological speculator, not the scientist he claims to be.

In this regard, a little history is relevant. In 1997, Plantinga and Peter van Inwagen issued a challenge to me. According to them, the Lehigh University biochemist Michael Behe's forthcoming book, *Darwin's Black Box,*[4] was a deeply serious, high-quality challenge to evolutionary theory, and my intellectual integrity as a Darwinian was on the line. Would I debate him? I took their endorsement seriously, and, not being a biochemist, asked for their permission to team up with somebody who knew the technicalities better than I did. I passed on their endorsement of Behe's book to my friend, the eminent Harvard evolutionary biologist David Haig, and he agreed to join me. When copies of the book arrived, we were appalled. This was not at all a serious science book, but hugely disingenuous propaganda, full of telling omissions and misrepresentations. We went to Notre Dame in April and dealt firmly, fairly, and objectively with Behe's claims, pointing out that his arguments were not just inconclusive; they gave every sign of willfully ignoring contrary evidence and argument. There was precious little rebuttal at that meeting in Notre Dame, and I figured that Haig and I had done our duty. I see that Plantinga no longer expresses any endorsement of Behe's first book, but now gives his layman's approval to his second book. I'm not biting. I've paid my dues.

Plantinga says, "If Behe is right, or anywhere near right, the probability of the existence of the cell as we find it is much greater on theism than on naturalism" (p. 9). Since

Plantinga is a layman, as he notes, he is really in no position to assess the antecedent of this claim: He finds the case that Behe makes is "reasonably powerful though far from conclusive." Where might an inquiring layman turn, then, for further guidance? He might turn to the scientific reviews, which have been uniformly devastating.[5] Or he might consider the following argument:

> Let B be "Behe is right, or anywhere near right."
> Let N be "Knowledgeable scientists rush to their labs to steal Behe's thunder and win the Nobel Prizes that will surely be awarded to anyone who demonstrates irreducible complexity."

Here then is my argument:

> $P(N/B)$ is very high. (Remember cold fusion?)
> N is false.
> ∴ P that Behe is right, or anywhere near right, is negligible.

But there is more to be said about this interesting case of a dog that isn't barking. There's one thing Michael Behe is right about: There are large gaps in our detailed accounts of the evolution of many complex features—for the trivial reason that it will take biologists centuries to investigate all the nooks and crannies of the biosphere. But more to the point, there are complex features—are they "irreducibly complex"?—that we know quite a bit about but still haven't much of a clue about how they evolved (if they did).

The question of how they evolved hasn't been studied for an interesting sociological reason: The young researchers who have the training to do it prefer to tackle other topics.

Why? Not because they fear that there is no evolutionary explanation of them, but for roughly the opposite reason. They fear that they would work hard for a decade, solve the problem, and show exactly how the features evolved, and hence are not, in spite of first appearances "irreducibly complex"—and their scientific colleagues would say, in effect, "What else is new? Of course they evolved. Thanks for proving something we never doubted in the first place." It's not just that most researchers, being prudent and cautious with their careers, prefer to work on the low-hanging fruit first, the topics that appear likely to produce significant results in a relatively short time, but that even those who are comfortable with the strategy of risking all for a Nobel Prize no matter how arduous and uncertain the prospect, are pretty sure that no Nobel Prizes are to be found down the ID pathways. That's how sure they are that the theory of evolution by natural selection is fundamentally confirmed. Of course they *might* be wrong, but who would advise them to risk wasting their professional careers on such a hunch?

That's why we should welcome the founding of Biologic, the Redmond, Washington, research entity (funded by the Discovery Institute) designed to house and fund those talented researchers—if such can be found—who think they *can* disprove the theory of evolution.[6] Let's hope they do first-rate science, and fill in a lot of the mildly embarrassing gaps in our knowledge of how various features evolved. If history is any guide, their quest for skyhooks will net them some interesting new cranes, and we'll all learn something. And in the meantime, we needn't lose any sleep over their spending their time on wild goose chases; they'll be on a crusade, and what could be more fulfilling than that, even if you come back empty-handed?

IV. Is naturalism incompatible with evolution?

What, finally, of Plantinga's argument that "naturalism is incompatible with evolution" (p. 17)? He's given the argument elsewhere, he says, so he can be brief. As he surmises, his first premise is the problematic one:

1. P(R/N&E) is low.

In everyday language, this says that the probability is low that our cognitive faculties are reliable, given naturalism and evolutionary theory. I have given the arguments against this premise elsewhere, and at great length, over more than thirty years, so I can be even briefer.[7]

Evolution by natural selection, with its naturalistic presuppositions, *explains why* hearts are highly reliable pumps, lungs are highly reliable blood oxygenators, eyes are highly reliable distal-information acquirers, and the beliefs that are provoked by those eyes (and other senses) are highly reliable truth trackers. I'm not sure what Pat Churchland meant when she said, "Truth, whatever that is, definitely takes the hindmost," but it shouldn't be taken to have the implication Plantinga puts on it. It is true that every belief state is what it is, and locally causes whatever it causes, independently of whether it is true or false. As I have said, our brains are *syntactic engines,* not *semantic engines,* which, like perpetual motion machines, are impossible. But syntactic engines can be designed to track truth, and that is just what evolution has done. A useful comparison might be with a hand calculator.

Arithmetical truth, whatever it is, definitely takes the hindmost, when it comes to what happens inside a hand calculator. For instance, it would be easy enough to design a bogus hand calculator that usually, or always, got its arithmetical answers wrong. Such a device is just as physically possible as a highly reliable calculator. But for obvious reasons, such devices have not been made. For the same sorts of reasons, unreliable empirical-belief calculators have not been generated by evolution. And in the case of *human* belief generation, we can add that cultural evolution over thousands but not millions of years has honed our belief-tracking systems by detecting and correcting dozens of blind spots and flaws discovered by…the very belief-tracking mechanisms that evolution endowed us with.

Descartes may have thought that we need God's benign intervention to have any trust in our cognitive abilities, but Descartes didn't have the benefit of Darwin's insights when he wrote (cf. my "Descartes's Argument from Design," *Journal of Philosophy* 2008).

NOTES

1. Daniel Dennett, "The Interpretation of Texts, People and Other Artifacts," *Philosophy and Phenomenological Research* (L, Supplement, 177–94, Fall 1990), 189–190.
2. Daniel Dennett, *Elbow Room* (Cambridge, MA: MIT Press, 1984), 149–50.
3. Jacques Monod, *Chance and Necessity* (New York: Knopf, 1971), 115.
4. Michael Behe, *Darwin's Black Box* (New York: Free Press, 1996).
5. See, for example, Sean B. Carroll, "Evolution: God as Genetic Engineer," *Science* (2007, June 8), 1427–1428; P. Z. Myers, http://scienceblogs.com/pharyngula/2007/06/behes_edge_of_evolution_part_i.php.
6. See *New Scientist* (2006, December 16), 9–11.

7. My arguments can be found in Daniel Dennett, *The Intentional Stance* (Cambridge, MA: MIT Press, 1987) and *Darwin's Dangerous Idea* (New York: Simon & Schuster, 1995). Among the others who have offered arguments along these lines are Elliott Sober, *From a Biological Point of View* (Cambridge University Press, 1994); Peter Godfrey Smith, *Complexity and the Function of Mind in Nature* (Cambridge Universtiy Press, 1996); and Kim Sterelny, *Thought in a Hostile World* (Oxford: Blackwell, 2003).

3

SUPERMAN VS. GOD?

Alvin Plantinga

I'd like to say first that I strongly suspect there is something in what I said that Dennett disagrees with. I'm having a little difficulty, however, in seeing just what it was. I rather enjoyed his silly stories about Superman and the really nasty art critic, and the like, but I'm not clear as to exactly how those stories were supposed to bear on what I said in my paper.

The organizers of this symposium asked us to address the question of whether religion and science are compatible. I argued that they are. I am happy to note that Dennett seems to agree. This agreement does come as something of a surprise, however, and seems to me to mark a significant

change from his book *Darwin's Dangerous Idea.*[1] I'm
delighted with the change; still, all is not yet sweetness
and light. While he agrees that religion and science, theism
and evolution, are compatible, Dennett goes on to point
out that many pretty silly propositions—for example, his
Supermanism—are also compatible with science.

When I first read Dennett's comment, I thought what
he had in mind is something like the following: Religion
and science are indeed compatible, but *many* silly propositions or positions are compatible with science, for example,
Supermanism. Theism, belief in God, is one of those silly
propositions that are compatible with theism. He puts it
like this: "I myself cannot see any rational grounds for preferring his [i.e., my] theism over my [i.e., his] Supermanism"
(p. 29).

On further thought, though, it struck me it wasn't
really theism he was claiming to be silly, but a different
proposition:

1. God guided and orchestrated the course of evolution
   to produce the kind of creatures he wanted.

I was arguing that God and evolution are possible, by
pointing to another proposition that is clearly possible, and
entails both the existence of God and the truth of evolution. That other proposition is 1; and I said that 1 was
possible. I wasn't arguing that 1 was *true,* but only using
it to show that the existence of God is compatible with the
current scientific theory of evolution. And 1 can do its job,
even if it isn't true, even if it isn't plausible, and even if it is
silly. All it has to be is possible. So Dennett's claim that 1 is
silly, like Supermanism, is wholly beside the point.

But maybe Dennett was thinking like this: If the *only* proposition that can be used to show that God and evolution are

compatible is a silly proposition, then one can believe that God and evolution are compatible only by believing a silly proposition. And maybe he thinks further that 1 *is* the only proposition that can be used in this way, and further, that 1 is silly—"Plantinga's particular *Genesis*-inspired *fantasy*" he calls it (ooo), and he thinks we shouldn't respect it.

Well, 1 is certainly *not* the only possible proposition that can be used in this way. But much more important, *why* does Dennett think 1 is silly? It doesn't seem even remotely silly to me; why does Dennett think it's silly? Apparently because he thinks it is relevantly like Supermanism, which we all agree is a foolish proposition.

Premise 1 doesn't seem to me to be at all like Supermanism. Supermanism is indeed silly; it isn't any more sensible than Dennettism, the idea that Dennett was actually present 500 million years ago and interfered with the course of evolution, intervened in it, and brought it about that there should now be the kinds of creatures we actually find. But of course Supermanism and Dennettism are silly in ways 1 isn't. For one thing, humanlike creatures like Superman and Dennett don't live nearly long enough; very few achieve an age of 500 million years. In fact Superman was brought up in the 1930s (in Kansas), and by now would be scarcely more than eighty years old. Dennett is even younger. And second, neither Superman nor Dennett is capable of relevantly intervening in the course of evolution. So Supermanism isn't at all relevantly like theism. Supermanism is a silly thesis; it doesn't in the least follow that theism is, or that the idea that God has guided and directed evolution is.

A couple more points. Dennett claims that *naturalism* is tacitly assumed in all reputable courts of law and throughout scientific investigation. If he is using the term "naturalism" the way I defined it in my paper, this is clearly and obviously false. In physics, for example, it is not assumed that there is no such person as God. There are very many physicists (perhaps 40 percent) who are also believers in God. These physicists do not take it that in doing physics they have to assume that there is no such person as God. Rather, what they think they are doing is exploring, explaining, and discovering how this world—a world that God has created—works. They believe that the world has been created by God; they take it that their job as physicists is to explore and understand God's handiwork. The hypotheses they propose may not directly entail the existence of God, but of course that doesn't mean they are assuming naturalism.

As for Michael Behe, let me say only that my recollection of his visit to Notre Dame is very different from Dennett's. Very different indeed. It does not seem to me that he was shown to be mistaken, let alone a charlatan. I thought he held his own very nicely with respect to Dennett and his friend.

I turn now to Dennett's comments on my evolutionary argument against naturalism (EAAN). First, he is right in suggesting that the creed I want to discredit is naturalism, not evolution. EAAN (naturally enough) is an argument against naturalism. But I must say I was disappointed in Dennett's response to this argument. What he does, basically, is to simply announce that evolution has in fact produced us, and that our beliefs do in fact track the truth. But that isn't the issue at all. I do not mean for a moment to argue that evolution has not produced us, or that our beliefs do not track the truth. Let me be clear: Our cognitive faculties are in fact reliable (our beliefs do in fact track the truth), and I have no objection to the thought that we have been produced by evolution. That isn't the issue at all.

The basic question is rather about the conditional probability that our faculties should be reliable, given naturalism and evolution. My premise 1 says that this probability is low. Most of my exposition of EAAN was devoted to an argument for 1, an argument to show that this probability is low. Sadly enough, Dennett doesn't even mention that argument; hence there is nothing here to reply to.

Dennett does propose an analogy, one I actually like very much. He likens us to calculators, which track the truth even though they are purely mechanical devices. This seems to me an unfortunate analogy from Dennett's point of view. Calculators, of course, are designed and created by intelligent beings, namely us human beings. Calculators track the truth, and do so precisely because they are *designed* to do so. This is just how a theist would think of human beings: They, too, track the truth because they were created and designed by an intelligent being. If we want to put EAAN into the context of Dennett's analogy, we would suppose that calculators reproduce themselves with occasional copy errors leading to different electronic designs. Some of these designs would be somehow adaptive with respect to their reproducing themselves. Furthermore, let's suppose these calculators produce shapes on a screen, as in fact they do, and finally, let's suppose these machines were not planned or designed by any intelligent beings at all. What would be the probability, on these suppositions, that the shapes on their screens are English sentences that express truths?

NOTE

1. Daniel Dennett, *Darwin's Dangerous Idea* (New York: Simon & Shuster, 1995).

4

HABITS OF IMAGINATION AND THEIR EFFECT ON INCREDULITY

Reply to Plantinga (Essay 2)

Daniel C. Dennett

Plantinga usefully draws attention to several points that I didn't emphasize in my first comments.

I

He finds my Superman story "silly," a "relatively foolish" proposition. After all, he reminds us, "humanlike creatures ... like

Superman don't live nearly long enough; very few achieve an age of 500 million years" (p. 41). Certainly it is foolish, on purpose. The question is this: Is it *relatively* foolish? Compared to his alternative? I would guess that the whole Superman scenario, with its kryptonite and x-ray vision, is probably at best only *logically* possible as philosophers so often like to insist—not self-contradictory, even though it violates sound scientific principles by the dozen. That was my point, since exactly the same verdict must be issued regarding virgin birth, walking on water, raising the dead, turning water into wine, and being resurrected from crucifixion. To anybody but a devout Christian, these are just as silly, just as foolish as Supermanism. If Plantinga were to claim that he himself had performed any of these feats, he would thereby destroy his own credibility. We know perfectly well that humanlike creatures and human beings can't do any such things.

He says he can't see why my Supermanism is *"at all like"* his proposition: "God guided and orchestrated the course of evolution to produce the kind of creatures he wanted." This is really interesting. It shows, I think, just how Plantinga's faith has, well, *disciplined* his imagination. He is so accustomed to imagining God as an intelligent agent without a body, and has so convinced himself that this makes some kind of sense, that he really can't see how similar the two stories are. God, like Superman, is intelligent, on the side of good, capable of amazing feats, and deeply interested in *Homo sapiens* on planet Earth. The chief differences are that Superman wears a cape and is *ripped.* In the question session following our talks, I was asked if it counted against my argument that hundreds of millions of people have believed one or another version of Plantinga's story while probably there are no believers of my Superman story. My answer is no. Plantinga's story was first assembled in an age of scientific ignorance, when almost nobody had the idea that the Earth was round, and no one had an inkling of its age, for instance. Today people are much better informed, but give me a few billion dollars to invest in Industrial Light and Magic chicanery and a few thousand years to let the story mellow, and we'll see how many Supermanists I can generate. Those Jor-el golden plates would certainly convince a lot of people—if not the National Academy of Science, but you know how conspiratorial those skeptical scientists can be! Add to that a Spielberg-directed "documentary" and we might really get the ball rolling. After all, roughly half a million people say they believe in the Angel Moroni's golden tablets. I rest my case.

Plantinga didn't hypothesize that Jesus guided and orchestrated the course of evolution; he hypothesized that God did. God is not Jesus, and maybe God can do things that Jesus can't do. I gather God wouldn't have to use hands and fingers and scientific instruments to "cause the right mutations to arise"; He could just arrange this by fiat. (Oh, but Jor-el could do that too, didn't I mention that? Jor-el's instructions were for his son Superman, who was more "humanlike" than his father.) It is clear, is it not, that whatever resources Plantinga uses to shore up his hypothesis are available to me to shore up my rival Supermanism. This is a mug's game.

I'm grateful to Plantinga for rising to the bait and criticizing my Superman story because my purpose, in case this wasn't obvious before, is to expose the intellectual shallowness of all such attempts to salvage consistency between science and religion by tweaking the creed until it is logically consistent with science. This is intellectual tennis without a net, and the fact that it is an ancient tradition with many eminent contributors does not make it more deserving of attention than any other mythology. It might be an amusing exercise to assign evolutionary roles to figures in the Greek or Roman pantheon—Poseidon could preside over the first 2 billion years, when life was restricted to the oceans; Aphrodite, with a wink, could provoke the evolution of sexual reproduction; and so forth. Supernatural and unfathomable beings automatically "can do" whatever our hearts desire, whatever our imaginations conjure up.

II

Plantinga says my claim that naturalism is tacitly assumed in all courts of law and throughout scientific investigation is "obviously false." "In physics, for example, it is not assumed that there is no such person as God (p. 42)." Really? Not even tacitly? When a physicist "proves" that a stone dropped from a height will fall with acceleration 9.8 meters/sec, does this not tacitly assume that no person (e.g., God) will intervene to adjust the rate? Physicists don't routinely add an escape clause, "unless God chooses to intervene," because it is tacitly assumed that no such "possibilities" are taken seriously. Here is what the great biologist, J. B. S. Haldane, said directly on this subject back in 1934:

> My practice as a scientist is atheistic. That is to say, when I set up an experiment I assume that no god, angel, or devil is going to interfere with its course; and this assumption has been justified by such success as I have achieved in my professional career. I should therefore be intellectually dishonest if I were not also atheistic in the affairs of the world.[1]

Courts of law follow the same naturalistic practice in their rules of evidence, and hence never confront issues like that posed in my little courtroom drama with Plantinga as expert witness. Naturalism is the *null hypothesis*. That means that it is always open to counsel to try to *demonstrate* that a miracle—some violation of naturalism—has occurred, but I wouldn't want my attorney to try the patience of a judge and jury with such a gambit.

In any case, Plantinga still has to decide whether he wants to defend Michael Behe as a naturalist or acknowledge, with Behe's critics, that he is a theological speculator, not an investigator playing by the rules of science. Behe claims to be a good naturalist, an investigator who uses the standard scientific methods to demonstrate irreducible complexity, and Plantinga's stout "defense" of Behe actually undermines him. It also supports a long-standing criticism I have made of the late Stephen Jay Gould's attempt at an ecumenical *détente* which Gould called NOMA: the doctrine of Non-Overlapping Magisteria that claims that science and religion deal with different, nonoverlapping issues, and hence can never properly be in conflict.[2] I don't buy it, and neither does Plantinga. He certainly sees the science of evolutionary biology as "overlapping" with his religious beliefs, enough to oblige him to cast about for a presentable refutation of that science, and he surely speaks for very many Christians (and Muslims, and others) when he expresses his discomfort with Darwinism. I think that only a deep conviction that Christianity *needs* Behe's proposition to be true could explain why as sophisticated a thinker as Plantinga would go out on such an unpromising limb. Even Kenneth Miller and Francis Collins, both practicing Catholics, have dismissed Behe as a crank. Can

Plantinga find a single reputable biologist who agrees with his opinion that Behe should be taken seriously?

When Gould, or more recently Michael Ruse, and Eugenie Scott of the National Center for Science Education, insist that there is really no necessary conflict between evolutionary biology and religion (properly understood), they persuade few devout Christians and Muslims. Plantinga speaks for the unpersuaded who know full well there is a conflict. In fact my disapproval of the NOMA gambit grows out of the worry that these attempts by well-meaning scientific diplomats do more harm than good, unwittingly convincing many laypeople that scientists will lie through their teeth to get evolution taught in the schools. Much better, in my opinion, is to say yes, there is a conflict, and once again, science wins (contra Plantinga).

Some Intelligent Design advocates have mischievously argued that if Dawkins and I are right that there is a conflict between evolutionary biology and religion, then evolutionary biology is a religion (in competition with other religions) and hence teaching it in schools is a violation of the First Amendment prohibition of government favoritism of any religion! By the same reasoning, of course, we would have to prohibit the teaching of modern astronomy and cosmology (where's Heaven?), modern physics (walking on water?), and nutrition (the loaves and the fishes?). We would also have to forbid teaching archeology and ancient history, which quite conclusively shows that the story of Exodus is a complete fabrication; there is no evidence that the Jews were ever expelled from, or even in, Egypt.

Christians had to abandon their earlier doctrines of Heaven when the Copernican revolution set in, and had to acknowledge that many of the stories in the Bible are not factual accounts but tall tales (more politely called myths) when historical and archeological research demonstrated their falsity. They now will have to abandon their doctrines of Creation. Some churches have long ago done just that, of course.

III

What about Plantinga's argument against naturalism? As he says, I ignore all but the first premise, which is, I think, obviously false, absolving me from considering the rest of the argument. Here is the first premise, in everyday words: The probability is low that our cognitive faculties are reliable, on the assumption of naturalism and current evolutionary theory. He says he gives an argument for this premise, which I didn't mention. Let's see. The argument is that belief states (given N and E) will be neural states of some kind, and in addition to their neural properties they will have content: A belief will be a belief that p, which can be true or false. There are three ways, Plantinga observes, that these properties can be related: by supervenience, either logical or nomological, or by identity (reductive materialism). That there are these three distinct possibilities for naturalism makes no difference to the argument since in each case, although (according to N and E) creatures with beliefs will have evolved to *behave* adaptively, they needn't *believe* truly. According to Plantinga, "natural selection doesn't give a fig for true belief just as such" (p. 19). The key claim is that a belief's "falsehood in no way interferes with the adaptivity of the NP [neurophysiological] properties" (p. 19) that somehow contribute to its realization. I did mention this claim, and dismissed it, and explained why. It is precisely the truth-tracking competence of belief-fixing mechanisms that explains their "adaptivity" in the same way that it is the blood-pumping competence of hearts that explains theirs.[3] Hearts are for circulating the blood and brains are for tracking the relevant conditions of the environment and *getting it right.*

IV

Finally, I would like to address Plantinga's rhetorical question about his imagined reproducing hand calculators. The thought experiment is too briefly sketched to evaluate, so let's put in a few details, so that we can see that Plantinga's imagination has let him down. Let's suppose that some calculators reproduce themselves, he says, with occasional copy errors leading to different electronic designs. "Some of these designs would be somehow adaptive with respect to their reproducing themselves" (p. 43). And, he goes on, suppose these calculators have screens on which symbols appear, and "let's suppose these machines were not planned or designed by any intelligent beings at all" (p. 43). Now, Plantinga asks, what would be the probability that the shapes on the screen express truths in English? One gathers that he thinks the answer is obviously, laughably low. But it all depends, of course, on how these devices earn a living. These calculators are going to have to get their electric power from somewhere, and since we human beings are the only concentrated source of electricity on the planet, they will have to be given it by us, or steal it from us. In other words, the calculators will have to be synanthropic—evolved to thrive in human company, like mice and cockroaches and bedbugs—whether or not we go on to domesticate them. They might earn their keep by wandering into the Game Boy Kingdom and providing us with entertainment of one sort or another—in which case there would be no need for their symbols to express *truths* (except within the fictions they depicted) but in mainly monoglot America there would be considerable selection pressure for the shapes on their screens to approximate English! If, on the other hand, they evolved to do serious informational work for us (competing with iPhones and Blackberries and the like), then whatever they do, they will have to get it right, in which case the probability that their symbols express truths will have to be about as high as (or higher than) a Blackberry running Wikipedia, for instance. That's a tall order, but is it flat out impossible? Plantinga apparently believes that such talented electronic agents simply could not evolve without a helping hand from intelligent design, but the plausibility of this conviction depends on historical happenstance, not on any known limitations on evolution. Given that intelligently designed devices of this ilk already exist in abundance, this would be a hard niche to invade, so it is no doubt highly unlikely that any such electronic devices could evolve *now* to compete successfully with those iPhones and Blackberries. For similar reasons, flying cats are unlikely to evolve *now,* since bats have already handsomely cornered the market for flying mammals. But there was a time when flying cats might well have evolved, either in competition with bats, or preempting the evolution of bats altogether. And there are several real-world instances of highly reliable *indicator species* that have coevolved with human beings. An instructive example is the honeyguide, a passerine bird that is not domesticated but nevertheless makes a living by leading human beings to wild beehives. If these birds weren't highly reliable, human beings wouldn't devote time and energy to following them, and leaving some of the found honey as payment for the birds, which cannot on their own break into the hives. A similar symbiotic relationship exists between some fishermen and oceanic birds, who get to feed on the bycatch, if only they can lead the boats to the schools of fish. It is not hard to imagine an arms race between different species of indicator birds, adding various informational "killer apps" to their talents, vying for human patronage. (Imagine a species of homing pigeon that earned its keep on ships by providing a sort of avian global positioning system that would lead the ship to its home port.) The fact that their *users* were intelligent beings who demanded a lot of them would not show that their *designer* had to be an intelligent being.

Anyone who has become familiar with any of the fruits of Artificial Life research, or genetic algorithms, knows that evolution *in silico* is not just a possibility; it is a practical reality. But could evolution in silico home in on truth tracking? Yes, of course. I take Plantinga's rhetorical question to be expressing a conviction that truth tracking simply could not evolve, in silico or in protein life forms, without a helping hand from intelligent designers, but if that is his view, it betrays a failure of imagination, not an insight into necessity, and of course it begs the question against our own evolution by natural selection, for surely *we* engage in truth tracking. To make an argument out of his example of the hand calculators, Plantinga would have to *demonstrate* that they could not home in on truth-tracking talents without the aid of intelligent designers, and that is going to require more than his expression of personal incredulity.

NOTES

1. J. B. S. Haldane, *Fact and Faith* (London: Watt's Thinker's Library, 1934).

2. Stephen Jay Gould, *Rocks of Ages: Science and Religion in the Fullness of Life* (New York: Ballantine, 1999).

3. If a more detailed explanation is sought, it can be found in Daniel Dennett, "Darwin's 'Strange Inversion of Reasoning'," *Proceedings of the National Academy of Science*, 106 (Suppl. 1), 10061–65.

5

Naturalism Against Science

Alvin Plantinga

I. Supermanism Again

According to Christopher Hitchens, "religion should be treated with ridicule, hatred and contempt."[1] Those who think like him ordinarily don't propose serious arguments against the truth of religious belief—theism for example; they prefer sneering condescension and mockery. I'm happy to say Dennett doesn't go along with Hitchens's "hatred and contempt"; he does, however, lean in the direction of ridicule.[2] For example, he and others like to try to discredit theism by comparing it with ideas everyone takes to be silly—Supermanism, or Flying Spaghetti Monsterism, or Tooth Fairyism, or Bertrand Russell's fantasy of an undetectable china teapot orbiting the sun, and so on. They typically don't give us their reasons (if they have any) for thinking theism is like these ideas. But *is* theism like these silly ideas? Well, any two views resemble each other in *some* respects. Take atheism and solipsism, for example. You are a solipsist if you think you are the only thing that exists, everything else being a figment of your imagination. Atheism obviously resembles solipsism in many ways: Both involve the denial of the existence of personal beings (atheism denies God; solipsism denies other persons); both go contrary to beliefs most people have and that furthermore we seem to be hard-wired to have; both are exceedingly hard to support by way of decent argument; etc.

As a matter of fact, atheism is a lot more like solipsism than theism is like Supermanism. Superman is certainly an impressive young fellow, but clearly not much greater than Captain Marvel, or even the Green Lantern. God, on the other hand, is all-knowing, all-powerful, and wholly good; furthermore, God has these properties essentially; he could not have been ignorant or impotent, or evil. He has also created the world.

Still further, according to classical theism, God is a *necessary being;* he exists in all possible worlds; it's not even possible that he should fail to exist. And since he has the property of being omniscient *essentially,* his believing a proposition is logically equivalent to that proposition's being true. Further yet, many theists hold that God's will, what he approves and disapproves, is the standard for right and wrong, good and bad. Superman may be faster than a speeding bullet and more powerful than a locomotive, but he is pretty small potatoes when compared with God.[3] (It's a little embarrassing to have to point out these obvious differences.)

Now of course we can modify the Superman story to make Superman more like God. We can change the story. We can say, in our revised Superman story, that Superman existed long before those boyhood days in 1930s Kansas; we can even say, if we like, that he has always existed. We could go further: We could say that Superman created the world. And we could add to his x-ray vision that he is omniscient (after all, the difference between x-ray vision and omniscience is only a matter of degree, not kind). Furthermore, not only is he more powerful than a locomotive: He is omnipotent—but, fortunately enough, perfectly good. We could say still further that Superman has these properties essentially. We could go further yet: We can declare him a necessary being. Combined with our claim that Superman is essentially omniscient, this means that a proposition's being true is logically equivalent to its being believed by Superman: Necessarily, grass is green if and only if Superman believes that grass is green.

If we did all this, then of course Dennett's claim that theism is like Supermanism would be true. In fact Supermanism (thus modified) would just *be* theism: "Supermanism" will be Dennett's idiosyncratic name for theism, and "Superman" will be his name for God. So theism is certainly like Supermanism, thus modified. And I guess we could do the same thing for the Flying Spaghetti Monster, the Invisible Pink Unicorn, Russell's teapot, the Tooth Fairy, and their ilk. Of course the problem for Dennett would then be that Supermanism and its relatives, now being identical with theism, would no longer be silly.

Richard Dawkins once complained that opponents of evolution sometimes resort to an argument from personal incredulity: They claim that the theory of evolution is false because they personally find it very hard to believe. Dennett and others make that same kind of argument from personal incredulity against theism. They find theism incredible, fantastic, irrational, worthy of ridicule and mockery, and so on. They don't typically give reasons (or if, like Dawkins, they do, they are exceptionally bad reasons): They just find it incredible. Of course they are entirely within their rights to do so: It's a free country. But why should the rest of us, those who find theism perfectly sensible and in fact believe it, as well as those of us who are on the fence between theism and atheism or naturalism—why should we be swayed by what Dennett and company do or don't find incredible? The vast bulk of the world's population find theism perfectly sensible; Dennett and his friends don't; why should the former be impressed by the latter?

As for myself, I'm not impressed. In fact it works just the other way on me. I find it extremely hard to believe that all the wonderful diversity of life on earth, including the human brain, should have come to be (as Dennett and his friends think they *have* come to be) by way of unguided evolution. I don't find it especially hard to believe that life should have come to be by way of Darwinian evolution—natural selection winnowing something like random genetic mutation; as I argued earlier, God could certainly have created the living world by using such a process. What is incredible is that the wonders of the living world should have come to be by *unguided* evolution. Those who believe that, but then raise their hands in self-righteous epistemic horror at the alleged epistemic excesses of theists, are like a bawdyhouse proprietor who is scandalized by the R-rated film shown in the theater next door.

II. Dennett's Dangerous Idea

In *Darwin's Dangerous Idea,* Dennett claims there is conflict between theism and current evolutionary theory.[4] Richard Dawkins concurs; indeed the subtitle of his *The Blind Watchmaker* is "How the Evidence of Evolution Reveals a Universe without Design."[5] In this they are mistaken; as conservative Christian theologians going back to the nineteenth century have argued, there is no conflict here.[6] Now it's bad enough to fall into serious intellectual error. This mistake, however, has important practical consequences as well: It harms both religion and science. It harms the former because it arrays the prestige of science against belief in God. But it also harms the latter. As has often been noted, fewer than one half of Americans accept the theory of evolution—the figure may be as low as 25 percent. No other theories in science—even such revolutionary heavyweights as quantum mechanics and relativity—excite a fraction of the public interest in the theory of evolution. Now why should this be the case? Americans don't ordinarily reject other basic scientific theses, such as relativity theory and quantum mechanics. True; they may not have heard much about these theories; but that just raises the question why evolution, as opposed to other central parts of science, is so much in the public consciousness.

The answer, of course, is obvious: It is because of the connection or entanglement of evolution with *religion.* Evolution is widely associated, in the popular mind, with *naturalism,* with a naturalistic, antireligious way of looking at the world; Americans tend to see evolution as the enemy of religion. Is this just due to fundamentalist confusion and ignorance? Hardly. They have excellent reason to do so: that choir of distinguished experts led by Dawkins and Dennett who tell us that evolution shows that in fact the universe is not designed. This choir doesn't stop at singing the praises of Darwinian evolution: They tell us that according to the theory of evolution, neither God nor any other agent has designed or created the living world. But of course that clearly contradicts a central and nonnegotiable tenet of the theistic religions, according to which God has indeed designed and created the world, including the living world. If indeed these experts are right (and since they are the experts, it is not wholly absurd to think they *are* right), then evolution is deeply incompatible with theistic religion, whether Christian, Jewish, or Muslim.

Now a solid majority of Americans are Christians, and many more (some 88 or 90 percent, depending on the poll you favor) believe in God. Moreover many of these believers are much more strongly inclined to accept theistic belief than the idea that all of the living world has come to be by unguided evolution. This latter idea isn't easy to stomach: According to Nobel Laureate Francis Crick, himself no believer in God, "Biologists must constantly keep in mind that what they see was not designed, but rather evolved."[7] Insofar as people associate evolution with naturalism, therefore, they are understandably suspicious of evolution—particularly since the scientific evidence for *unguided* evolution (as opposed to evolution *simpliciter*) seems to be scant to nonexistent.

Given this alleged connection between evolution and naturalism, furthermore, many Americans are understandably reluctant to have evolution taught to their children in the public schools, the schools they themselves pay taxes to support. Protestants don't want Catholic doctrine taught in the schools and Christians don't want Islam taught; but the distance between naturalism and theistic belief, whether

Catholic or Protestant, or Muslim or Jewish, is vastly greater than the distance between Catholics and Protestants or, for that matter, between Christians and Muslims. Christians, Jews, and Muslims concur on belief in God; naturalism stands in absolute opposition to these theistic religions; and evolution is widely seen as a pillar in the temple of naturalism. This association of evolution with naturalism is the obvious root of the widespread antipathy, in the United States, to the theory of evolution. Insofar as Dennett and others proclaim conflict between evolutionary theory and theistic belief, they exacerbate this distrust of evolution—a distrust that spills over to science itself, with a consequent cost in public support of science. The health and welfare of science is therefore damaged by promoting these myths to the effect that current evolutionary theory is in conflict with theistic religion. Of course that's not much of a reason for those who believe those myths to stop promoting them. What it does mean, though, is that there is very good reason for exposing them for the myths they actually are: the damage they do to science.

III. Naturalism

The word *naturalism* is used in many different ways. In my original piece I defined it as follows: Naturalism is the view that there is no such person as God or anyone like God. It is naturalism so understood that I mean to argue against. Contrary to Dennett, furthermore, naturalism so taken is obviously *not* assumed either in science or in courts of law. In science, we assume that God won't capriciously interfere with our experiments. The same goes in everyday life: I'm rock climbing and reach for a hold; I take it for granted that God won't turn that hold into Jell-O just as I touch it.

J. B. S. Haldane seems to think this assumption amounts to atheism. But why think a thing like that? Can't one believe in God, a God who can act in the world, and also assume that God won't arbitrarily interfere with experiments? Some 40 percent of scientists believe in God and believe that he can act in the world; no doubt they also make the assumption that God won't arbitrarily interfere with their experiments. According to legend, Galileo dropped cannonballs of different weights off the Tower of Pisa to test Aristotle's theory that heavy objects fall faster than light objects. Historians tell us this legend is false: Perhaps Giambattista Benedetti performed that experiment. No matter; whoever performed it, no doubt he assumed that God would not capriciously adjust the rate of fall.

But that's a very long way from atheism or naturalism.[8] Haldane seems to think intellectual honesty requires him to be an atheist (given that he assumes God won't interfere with his experiments); as far as I can see, that's like thinking intellectual honesty requires me to deny the existence of my children, given that I assume they won't set my house on fire. There is an enormous difference between atheism and assuming that God won't interfere with my experiments. (Or are we to suppose that what we have here is a shiny new argument for atheism? "If there were such a person as God, he could spoil my experiment; nothing can spoil my experiment; therefore....")

Indeed, one of the ways in which Christian theism is hospitable to science, one of the reasons modern empirical science came to be and flourished in the Christian West, is this assumption that God is in control of nature and does not act arbitrarily. According to Christian, Jewish, and some varieties of Islamic theism, God has created us human beings in his image. For present purposes, we can

take this to mean that he has created us as rational creatures, creatures who resemble him in having the capacity
to know important things about ourselves, our environment, and God himself. The divine image includes more:
It includes a moral sense, a grasp of right and wrong, and
the ability to know and love God. But a central and crucial
part of the divine image in us human beings is our ability to have worthwhile and important knowledge about
ourselves and our world. Obviously our ability to do science is an extremely important part of the divine image, so
taken. God has created both us and our world, and created
them in such a way that the former can know much about
the latter. But this implies that God would not arbitrarily
stand in the way of our coming to such knowledge—by, for
example, capriciously spoiling our experiments. And this
shows, as against Dennett and Haldane, how far off the
mark is the suggestion that science presupposes atheism
or naturalism.

Of course God's faithfulness and reliability along these
lines doesn't mean that he never acts in ways outside of
the normal course of things: It doesn't mean, for example,
that miracles never occur. Some people seem to think
that the occurrence of miracles, supposing they occurred,
would somehow go against science—presumably because
miracles would violate the laws promulgated by science. I
don't have the space here to go into this matter properly,[9]
but this too is error. The important point here is that
the laws or principles of science are typically stated for
closed systems, systems that are closed to outside causal
influence. Thus "This is the principle of conservation of
linear momentum: *When no resultant external force acts
on a system,* the total momentum of the system remains
constant in magnitude and direction."[10] And the principle

of conservation of energy states that "the internal energy of an isolated system remains constant. This is the most general statement of the principle of conservation of energy."[11] But now suppose God miraculously created a full-grown horse inside the headquarters of the American Association for the Advancement of Science: Any system containing that headquarters, obviously, would not be causally closed; hence the preceding principles would not apply to them.

IV. EAAN

Finally, I turn once more to EAAN, the evolutionary argument against naturalism. Dennett and other Brights seem to think the naturalists can refute this argument by basically ignoring it, announcing in an airy (or condescending) line or two that they don't believe the conclusion. No doubt they don't, but that's no way to refute an argument.[12] We might perhaps expect Dims to carry on in this way; one expects better of Brights.

A central premise of the argument (see earlier, pp. 17) is that the probability of our cognitive faculties' being reliable, given naturalism and evolution, is low: P(R/N&E) is low. I'll conclude by saying a bit more about the argument for this premise, which is perhaps the central premise of the argument.

In the first place, of course, my claim is certainly not that our cognitive faculties are unreliable, or that it is probable that they are. I believe, of course, that our cognitive faculties—memory perception, a priori insight, Reid's sympathy, whereby we know what others are thinking and feeling—I believe that these faculties are indeed reliable. That is not to say that we never hold false beliefs: Obviously we often do. Nor is it to say that there are no areas where we are subject to cognitive illusions of one sort or another: Some have claimed, for example, that we very easily fall into error in making probability judgments. (Even there, of course, those who make this claim believe that *they* are able to make the relevantly correct probability judgments.) Moreover, on many topics, being able to hold accurate opinions isn't easy; it requires discipline and training.

Second, I'm not denying that we and our cognitive faculties have come to be by way of evolution—natural selection winnowing random genetic mutation, for example. Like any theist, I don't think we have come to be by way of *unguided* evolution; but that's a wholly different matter.

What I do claim, however, in this crucial first premise, is that the conditional probability of our faculties being reliable, *given naturalism and evolution,* is low. (As I said earlier, I am including materialism with respect to human beings in naturalism.) The argument is straightforward. As I said in my initial statement, if materialism is true, a belief will be a neurophysiological structure of some kind—a group of neurons connected together in a certain way. This belief will have two kinds of properties: neurophysiological properties (NP properties) and a *content* property: The belief will be the belief that p for some proposition p, in which case p will be the content of the belief. NP properties are *physical* properties; the property of having such and such a content is a *mental* property. Materialists hold that mental properties are identical with physical properties (reductive materialism) or that mental properties are determined by physical properties, in that for every mental property M, there is a physical property P such that necessarily, if a structure has P, it also has M. The necessity here can be either broadly logical or causal.

Now the NP properties of a belief can cause behavior—adaptive or maladaptive as the case may be. Natural selection selects for adaptive behavior and against maladaptive behavior. In so doing, it also selects for adaptive neurophysiology: It selects for NP properties that cause adaptive belief and against NP properties that cause maladaptive behavior. Now the content of a belief is determined by these NP properties. In my initial statement I suggested we think about some other population of creatures for whom N and E hold: We may assume that the NP properties of their beliefs are adaptive.

But what about the *truth* of those beliefs? We know that the content of their beliefs (and of course what makes a belief true [or false] is that it has true [or false] content) is determined by the NP properties of that belief. A given content is caused or determined by a given set of NP properties. What evolution selects for is adaptive behavior and adaptive NP properties; but as for the content, that is determined by a given set of adaptive NP properties, and evolution just has to take potluck (not that it minds). Evolution just has to put up with the content that is determined by the particular NP properties in question. And the point is, it doesn't matter to the adaptivity of those NP properties, whether the content they determine is true or false. Those NP properties cause adaptive behavior; they also determine belief content, but we have no reason to think the belief content true. If it's true, fine; but if it's false, that's equally fine.

Here's an objection: Wouldn't the content have to be true for the organism to behave appropriately? Suppose the belief content associated with a given set of NP properties is false: Wouldn't that lead to maladaptive behavior?

Suppose one of those creatures believes that amanitas mushrooms (which are poisonous) are good to eat: Won't that lead to behavior incompatible with survival? So don't we have to posit true beliefs on the part of those creatures to *explain* their adaptive action?

Not at all. Think about a frog sitting on a lily pad: A fly buzzes past, the frog's tongue flicks out and nails the fly. Does it matter what the frog then believes, if indeed frogs have beliefs? Clearly not: What matters is the frog's behavior and the neurophysiology that causes that behavior. Of course *something* in the frog registers or indicates the approach of the fly, the distance from fly to frog, the velocity of the fly, and so on; and those somethings are part of the cause of the frog's capturing the fly. Call those structures *indicators*. For the frog's behavior to be adaptive, for it to capture the fly, it is necessary that there be indicators, and necessary that they indicate accurately. But none of that need involve *belief*. The frog doesn't have to believe that the fly is such and such a distance away, flying at such and such a velocity, and so forth; it doesn't so much as have to believe that there is a fly present.

In the same way, there are also indicators in a human body, various structures that indicate or register various states of affairs in the body, and cause appropriate reactions. Elements of the immune system may register the presence of foreign bodies, perhaps microbes involved in an infection; this will cause a response designed to destroy the invasive agents. But of course neither the immune system, nor any part of it, nor the person whose body is in question need believe that the body has been invaded by infection-causing microbes. There are structures that register the presence of infection and cause a fever (antibodies can do their thing better at a higher temperature); again, nothing in the neighborhood—the immune system, the antibodies, the person sustaining the infection—need form any beliefs. Indeed, the person in question may believe that he or she *doesn't* have an infection.

Adaptive behavior requires accurate indicators: The frog will capture the fly only if the relevant indicators in the frog are indicating accurately. The explanation of the frog's adaptive behavior is that the relevant indicators accurately register the relevant states of affairs. But as we've just seen, of course, indication is not belief. And if indication is going properly, it doesn't matter what the organism in question believes. We don't need to posit true beliefs in the frog to account for its adaptive behavior: what is required is only accurate indication; and accurate indication need not be accompanied by true belief. As long as the indication is accurate, the belief content can be anything whatever. This objection to the argument therefore fails.

By way of conclusion, there isn't any conflict between Christian belief and science in the area we've been investigating. Christian belief and evolutionary science are entirely compatible. Perpetuating the myth that there is conflict, furthermore, is harmful both to religion and to science. The fact is theistic belief, with its teaching of God's creating human beings in his image, is eminently friendly and receptive to science. On the other hand, there *is* conflict between naturalism and science, in that one can't rationally accept both naturalism and evolution. But evolution is one of the pillars of contemporary science; hence there is deep conflict between naturalism and science. Still further, there are no good reasons to accept or believe naturalism; and there are powerful reasons, including the evolutionary argument against naturalism, to reject it. Naturalism, therefore, is intellectually bankrupt. If this is the best Brights can do, I think I'll stick with the Dims.[13]

NOTES

1. Christopher Hitchens (University of Toronto lecture, 2009).
2. For a particularly egregious example, see Daniel Dennett, *Darwin's Dangerous Idea* (New York: Touchstone, 1995), 164.
3. These are ways in which Superman is unlike God. Supermanism is also unlike theism, belief in God. For example, there are a number of reasonably strong arguments for the existence of God; at last report there were none for the existence of Superman. Many accept theism; hardly any accept Supermanism.
4. "An impersonal, unreflective, robotic, mindless little scrap of molecular machinery is the ultimate basis of all the agency, and hence meaning, and hence consciousness, in the universe." Dennett, *Darwin's Dangerous Idea*, 203.
5. Richard Dawkins, *The Blind Watchmaker* (New York: W. W. Norton & Co., Inc., 1986).
6. As Dennett seems to concede in his earlier response (p. 26) to my original statement.
7. Francis Crick, *What Mad Pursuit: A Personal View of Scientific Discovery* (New York: Basic Books, 1988), 138.
8. It might be closer to what is often called *methodological* naturalism, but methodological naturalism is certainly not the naturalism under discussion here.
9. But see Alvin Plantinga, "What Is 'Intervention'?," *Theology and Science*, 6: 369–401.
10. Francis W. Sears and Mark W. Zemansky, *University Physics* (Boston: Addison-Wesley, 1963), 186 (emphasis added).
11. Sears and Zemansky, *University Physics*, 415 (emphasis added).

12. For (by contrast) a serious and responsible response to EAAN by a nontheist, see Michael Tooley's reply in Alvin Plantinga and Michael Tooley, *Knowledge of God* (Oxford, UK: Blackwell, 2008) 184ff; see also the essays in James Beilby, *Naturalism Defeated?* (Ithaca, NY: Cornell University Press, 2002).

13. My thanks to Brian Boeninger, Kenny Boyce, Nate King, Marcin Iwanicki, and Anne Peterson.

6

NO MIRACLES NEEDED

Daniel C. Dennett

According to an oft-told story, an aeronautical engineer once proved from first principles that bumblebees simply cannot fly. I was reminded of this legend[1] by Plantinga's argument, purporting to prove that naturalism defeats itself: that epistemic agents who were the products of (mere) evolution by natural selection would, by the very fact of their modest lineage, have no warrant to trust their own judgment. I don't suppose the aeronautical engineer was trying to demonstrate that the flight of the bumblebee is a miracle (although of course it might be—it's *logically* possible, as some philosophers love to say!). I expect the intent was to demonstrate the shortcomings in the aeronautical principles relied on: "Something must be wrong with my argument, since there goes the bumblebee!" Plantinga, in contrast, does want to use his argument to demonstrate that our manifest competence as truth trackers—our capacity to fly as scientists, you might say—is grounds for believing that a miracle must have happened. According to Plantinga's argument, an Intelligent Designer has had a hand (well, not literally a *hand,* but a divine nudge of some kind) in our evolution, since such a competence as we exhibit could not otherwise come to exist. This is apparently his attempt to shore up Michael Behe's forlorn argument from irreducible complexity with his own version, replacing the bacterial flagellum with human cognitive competence.

The argument is indirect. The last sentence of Plantinga's opening essay is "The real conflict is between evolution, that pillar of contemporary science, and *naturalism*" (p. 21). His idea is that if unguided natural selection could not give us grounds for trusting our cognitive competence, and our cognitive competence is just as obvious as the flight of the bumblebee, then we are supposedly constrained to abandon our naturalism and grant God a role in vouchsafing this cognitive competence to us. There is no doubt in Plantinga's mind that we human beings can discern the truth, and know that we are doing so, and indeed, this is assumed on all sides by the very activity of engaging in reasoned inquiry. Why would we devote time and energy to it if we didn't think we were capable of doing it?[2] So something must give: either naturalism or Plantinga's argument.

Plantinga apparently thinks that he has shown first that there is room in evolutionary biology (minus naturalism) for the hypothesis that a theistic God intervened, and second that God must have taken advantage of that room, intervening at the appropriate moments in our evolutionary history and tweaking the processes that gave us the capacity to do science (and, of course, to worship our creator). A purposeless, unguided evolutionary process just could not achieve the same results.

Plantinga wanted to show, in other words, that science and religion are not just compatible: Science *depends on theism* to underwrite its epistemic self-confidence. If the only creatures under consideration were, say, snails, frogs, and dolphins, the claim would be granted on all sides that the epistemic talents provided them by natural selection are too crude and practical to grant them reliable visions of science. But unlike these simpler animals, we multiply our epistemic talents by orders of magnitude, thanks to cultural evolution and the sharing of methods, tools, and perspectives that it enables. As Bo Dahlbom once put it, "You can't do much carpentry with your bare hands and you can't do much thinking with your bare brain."[3] Our brains are far from bare. We have developed and proven the reliability of dozens of prosthetic extensions of our native cognitive talents. Our capacity to discover the facts, and to have good reasons for believing that we have done so, is explicable without appeal to inexplicable or irreducible genius, immaterial minds, or a divine helping hand. The passage from intelligent hominid to language-using *Homo sapiens* to scientist is one that we are only beginning to uncover, so we cannot yet *prove* that there are no miracles along the way, but the burden of proof lies on the other side. Let Plantinga, like Behe, try to show us the irreducible complexity in our minds that could not possibly have evolved (by genetic and cultural evolution). He will find, as Behe has, that his inability to imagine how this is possible is not the same as a proof that it is impossible.[4]

Richard Dawkins calls this the Argument from Personal Incredulity, and it is an obvious fallacy.

I have shown that Plantinga's argument depends on a false premise, so we can continue to pursue our naturalistic evolutionary science without miracles. We no doubt have some limitations on what we can understand, and there are surely many facts forever beyond our ken, but this does not show that there is some fatal flaw, some epistemological original sin that cripples our attempts to know, but just that we are finite creatures with a finite evolutionary history.

NOTES

1. The story appears to have some foundation in fact, though it has been transformed through retelling, a meme with quite a distinguished history, dating back to the 1930s, when August Magnan, a famous French entomologist, and his lab assistant, M. Saint-Lague, did the engineering calculations, as reported in Magnan's book, *Les Vols des Insects* (Paris: Hermann, 1934). Of course Magnan realized that this was a *reductio* of current thinking in aeronautical engineering. See also John McMasters, 1989, "The Flight of the Bumblebee and Related Myths of Entomological Engineering," *American Scientist*, 77: 164–68.

2. Roger Wertheimer developed this point in his *The Significance of Sense* (Ithaca: Cornell University Press, 1974), 110–11.

3. Bo Dahlbom (unpublished).

4. In Behe's account of the bombardier beetle (*Darwin's Black Box*, New York: Free Press 1996, 35–36), and in his speculations about how flagella might have evolved (65–66), he raises interesting possibilities, and grants that "All we can conclude at this point is that Darwinian evolution *might* have occurred" (36). And as he himself admits, "The frustrating answer is that

we can't tell" (41). In the end, he says, he finds it "extremely implausible" that evolutionary accounts of these phenomena will be forthcoming. That is an autobiographical confession, not a scientific demonstration. (And as scientists have shown, Behe's incredulity is not shared, since there is a wealth of evidence concerning how (and when, and why) these putatively "irreducibly complex" features did in fact evolve.)

INDEX